The 21-Day Self-Confidence Challenge

An easy and step-by-step approach to overcome self-doubt & low self-esteem and start developing solid self-confidence

21 Day Challenges

The 21-Day Challenges
Kindle & Paperback

Happiness

Self-love

Self-Confidence

Mindfulness

Stress Management

Minimalism

Productivity

Budgeting

Exercise

Weight Loss

Clean Eating

Introduction

I used to have a friend in university, let's call her the most glamorous name I can think of, "Marie Claire". Marie Claire was beautiful in that way you try to be irritated about but can't, because she also happened to be mind-numbingly nice and friendly. She was kind, considerate, deeply intelligent, funny, creative and hard working. All the girls wanted to be Marie Claire, all the boys wanted to be with her, and all the lecturers wanted to give her an A for all her classes, just for pitching up.

One day, Marie Claire and I got drunk together near the end of semester. Because she only ever did things perfectly, we had been drinking bottles of promotional champagne she had been given from one of her part time modeling gigs. The conversation turned serious as the evening grew late, and eventually, she looked into my eyes and told me that actually, she had always felt very, very ugly growing up. She confessed to hating the way she looked, hating who she was and wishing everyday she could be someone else, someone better.

I was flabbergasted, and not just because I had been steadily putting away more than my fair share of champagne. I was shocked because I had just assumed she was perfectly happy, always confident, worry free. In fact, what I heard her saying sounded suspiciously like the kind of thing *I* would have complained about.

That night I thought hard about what it means to be confident. I had always assumed that if I just magically managed to be as awesome as someone like Marie Claire, the confidence would naturally follow. But what did it mean if even *she* felt unconfident at times? It was depressing, at first, but after a while I realized - self-confidence is all a state of mind. I realized that people seem to think that self-confidence is a result of success in life, or only for those who "deserve" it. But that evening I saw evidence that that couldn't be true. Instead, self-confidence is something you have to work at and protect and nurture just like anything else. That self-confidence comes from *within*.

Day 1: What would you do if you were infinitely confident?

Lets start this challenge with a thought experiment. Take a moment to imagine yourself, only a supremely confident version. If you have a ridiculous imagination like I do, you might like to really run with this and have fun. If you had zero body hang ups, no doubts about your value as an employee, no worries about your innate lovability and no second guesses as to how good your karaoke really was and whether people have just been lying to you this whole time ...what would things look like?

Don't get caught on the details, just enjoy the visuals for a moment. Maybe you'd waltz up to that cute guy at the bar and try your cheesiest pickup line on him simply because you trusted that you were basically a charming person. Maybe you'd spontaneously sing out loud that song you have in your head because you like it, and because you're happy, and because you have a good voice dammit, and why not?

Maybe the next time your aunt gives you industrial strength deodorant for Christmas you can smile and not give even a tiny damn because you know, deep down, that you're great as you are and that it's not your problem if people want to be passive aggressive with you. Maybe - and this is a big one! - maybe when somebody says "your hair looks nice today" you would smile and say thank you because, well, your hair *does* look nice.

Think of how you'd be at work, at home, with those you love and those you don't. Think of all the things you'd do differently. Imagine yourself saying and thinking all those things, now, in detail.

Now, this is the important thing: *you can feel this way right now*.

Yup. Just like my beautiful and wonderful friend Marie Claire somehow managed to feel like crap, you can also feel confident *without* having to be a genius supermodel with a trust fund. In fact, you can feel brave and confident and full of a sense of your own self esteem right now, just as you are.

What's your reaction to that? If you're like most people, it's something along the lines of "psssh, yeah right!"

In our culture, and especially for those who've been raised that way, the idea that we can be confident in ourselves and our worth and our abilities just by default seems pretty stupid. While everyone can agree that it's great to have self-confidence, we generally imagine it's only reserved for those special people who've earned it, and that yeah yeah, we'll get there someday. Right now? We find it hard to drum up any love for ourselves at all. On that note, lets move onto the next exercise...

Day 2: Where are you now?

Have you noticed that most children seem to bounce into this world with a really hefty amount of self-esteem? Really. If you've ever chatted to a kid about their crappy crayon drawing or pasta art, you'll immediately see that there's no pretend humility, no self-effacement. Just pride and confidence. Ask them what they want to be and they'll tell you "a unicorn trainer" or some other harebrained thing without the least sense of irony.

But people grow up and get the shine knocked out of them, and most teenagers, especially after a few years in the public education system, not only *don't* have confidence in themselves, they actively doubt their own worth. Chat to fully grown adults and many of them have abandoned their dreams long ago, feel average on even their best days and have a steady stream of negative self talk playing on in their heads almost constantly.

Grim!

How do you measure up when it comes to self-confidence? Before we move on and take a measuring tape to our own sense of self worth, let me clarify what I mean by confidence in the first place. You know that arrogant bastard at work who thinks he's right even when (or especially when!) he's wrong? Yeah, he's not what I mean. You know that friend you have who basically has a stroke whenever you criticize him? I don't mean that, either. Your awkward cousin who doesn't seem to understand that his mixed media art pieces posted on Facebook are making the family uncomfortable ...he's not confident either.

Then what *is* confidence?

Well, when you're confident, you have a solid, realistic sense of who you are. And no matter what that is, you have a set level of love and respect that you give yourself just for free, for no reason. Behind self-confidence is joy, happiness, acceptance and compassion. But behind arrogance is fear, resentment and stress. See if you can feel the difference:

Arrogance: "I'm a real, curvy women, and you skinny bitches better bow down"
Confidence: "I've got a big build and a few extra pounds, and that's OK. I'm working on slimming down, but I'm also working on loving exactly who I am right now"

Arrogance: "They don't understand me. They're too boneheaded to truly grasp my vision anyway, no wonder they hate it"
Confidence: "They may have a point. Maybe my proposal could have been better. But I'm still a valuable team member and I will produce something better next time"

Arrogance: "I secretly think our relationship is better than most other people's relationships"
Confidence: "You never know what will happen in the future, but I'm grateful she's in my life, and I'm confident that whatever happens, we'll always be on good terms with each other"

So, it's not necessary to be perfectly skilled at something to feel confident about your abilities. It's not necessary to be in complete control, to be "winning", to be successful. To be confident, you only need to have a firm core in yourself, a grasp of your value that cannot be altered with external circumstances. For example the last point - you can be a good husband or boyfriend, even though you have a failed relationship. You can be confident in your ability to always strive to be a better partner, in yourself, no matter how your circumstances actually play out.

Today's exercise: how confident are you? On a piece of paper, jot down a number on a scale of one to ten to indicate how confident you feel, with 10 being "completely" and 1 being "I usually wish I was invisible". Decide on a number for all of the following areas: love and relationships, work and career, physicality, personality, and achievements. To help you decide on a number for each of these areas, try answering the following questions for each category. The more you answer "yes" to, the higher score you can give yourself.

- You find it easy to accept a compliment in this area

- If someone insults you about this area, you shrug it off because you know it's not really true (or it's true and you accept the fact)

- A failure in this area would be unfortunate, but not the end of the world

- You feel like you can clearly say what you are and are not capable of in this area

- You feel like you do what you do in this area because you *want* to

- You judge yourself on your *own* standards in this area, not anybody else's

- You feel confident enough to learn from your mistakes, when you make them

As you measure up, are you surprised by anything? Saddened or proud of anything? Pick your one or two lowest scores and have a look - have they always been this way? When did you lose confidence in this area? Why?

Lastly, ask yourself honestly what your life will look like if you continue to go out into the world with your confidence levels where they are. Think *clearly* of all the opportunities you'll miss, of the avenues you won't pursue, of the opportunities you'll pass by and the joy that will be invisible to you.

Are you willing to commit to changing all this, if you don't like the picture of the future it paints? Confidence is a bit like a key: with it, certain things just open up. When you are happy, open and self-assured, the world responds. Really, it does. People are more open and trusting, and begin to treat you accordingly. When you act as though you treat yourself very well, other people are usually keen to treat you the same way. Are you willing to commit to making the change?

Day 3: You're more awesome then you give yourself credit for

I'm not asking you to blindly love *everything* about yourself, all the time, no matter what, even if those things are really flawed. That serves nobody, and is not really any different from hating everything about yourself no matter what.

We all know that annoying girl who's read too much girl-power literature who wants to affirm the hell out of everything. You know the kind - she calls herself a goddess; she write poems to her stretchmarks and whatever you say (really, whatever you say), she responds with something like, "Wow! That's so interesting! You have such a valuable and unique contribution, Thank you so much for suggesting that we go get falafel for lunch today, that is an *absolutely awesome* suggestion. Man, you're really killing it today." Nobody really likes (or trusts!) this sort of phoniness, and it's not necessary either.

Instead, the kind of self-confidence we'll be building in this book is a little more subtle, a little more resilient, and is much less annoying to the general population! Today's exercise is to list some of our qualities that deserve more love than we've maybe been giving them. When you're a little kid, your teacher praises you half to death if you can remember to put your coat away in the locker, but everyone expects you to have that down by the time you're an adult. In fact, it sometimes seems to me that the moment people have mastered or achieved something, the bar is simply put higher and they're just expected to do more.

Let's try to remember all the things that make us awesome.

I bet you can't think of one person right now in your friend group or family who is completely without redeeming qualities (well, except for our girl power girl above, we'll forget about her for now). Well, you also have redeeming qualities, even if you've forgotten about them!

It's time to make an inventory of things that we can love and value about ourselves, and that others love and value about us, too. As you do this, you may feel a little uncomfortable. Especially if you're female, you may have received extensive boot camp training in the university called life about how *not* to love yourself ...but try anyway.

Today, as you make this list, your other, hidden goal is to watch how you respond to the task. Do you secretly think, "yeah yeah that's nice but I don't *really* believe any of this crap" or "I have nice eyes but wow do I ever hate my chewed up fingernails ...so I guess they cancel each other out or something"? Do you hear the critical voice of a parent or ex arguing with you? Do you feel silly or uncomfortable? Just become curious about your reaction.

- List 5 physical qualities that you like about yourself. They can be big things (you love your whole body, you beat cancer) or little, strange things (every boyfriend has loved the wrinkle your nose makes when you laugh)

- List 5 personal qualities you like about yourself (the patience of a stoned saint, creativity, trustworthiness...)

- List 5 (or more!) achievements you are proud of (raising your children, earning your degree, building your yacht from scratch)

- List 5 things you've done which someone else might not have had the courage to do

And that's it. We don't have to pick those apart yet, or analyze them, or give our monkey brains too much of an opportunity to argue back. Just put it down, out there in the world, and feel what it feels like to have good, lovable qualities.

Day 4: Finding - and busting out of - your comfort zone

Ah, comfort zones. Don't they sound lovely? Maybe yours has cats and Netflix and ice cream sandwiches in it. Maybe in your comfort zone, everyone is nice and non-judgmental. Maybe you're not expected to work hard or struggle or try new things. It's really cool, everything stays the same all the time and nothing ever changes. Uh. I mean. Actually that last bit sounds kind of boring, doesn't it?

The trouble with safety, as lovely as it is, is that it's *dead*. Life is a strange, always changing, sometimes scary beast, and finding a little safe space inside it is, well, artificial. Nothing in life improves without leaving that safe, boring comfort zone. When you settle inside a comfort zone, you are making a choice, and the choice sounds like this, "I don't know what's out there, but I'm unprepared to take a risk and go and see, rather I'll just stick with what I have already, it might not be as good, sure, but at least I don't have to do any work to get it!"

Yeah, sounds lame, right?

Now, your ice cream sandwich is just a mess without the two cookies holding everything together, and boundaries and limits are fabulous things to have for the same reason. But sometimes you get too comfortable in your comfort zone. It becomes a *boredom* zone. You stay there not because it's a space you feel happiest in, but because you're too scared to explore other spaces.

For now, whatever your comfort zone is ("I have a low self esteem, I've always had one, sigh! That's just the way I am"), well, you can come back to it later. Send out your little psychological feelers to find that "stretch zone" just outside of that. Here, you are acting, thinking and feeling in ways that are new enough to be interesting but not so new that you lose your nerve and run back to your safe zone with your tail between your legs.

Where this zone actually is will be up to you to decide. A little fear? Fantastic. A little apprehension? Great. Feeling like you're going to throw up and pass out from anxiety? Probably less fantastic. Your mileage may vary, of course, but as long as you're pushing yourself, it's all good.

Drawing up a map to leave your comfort zone

Alright, happy traveller, here we go. You're going to boldly go where your self-confidence has never gone before, and yeah, it's going to feel a bit funny at first. Lets start big and get a feel for the lay of the land. Look at the year lying ahead of you. Choose 12 (1 for each month) goals that will bring you out of what is safe and ordinary and boring for you. These are all the things you imagined you could do if you had confidence, remember?

Make them doable, but make them big and quite challenging. Going to a nude beach in the dead of summer. Submitting your short story to that magazine. Leaving the job that makes you feel bad about yourself. Introducing yourself to that person who's been on your mind all this time. You get the idea.

Now, put those aside and zoom in further. For the next month, pick one of those challenges to work your way up to. By the end of this challenge, my hope is that you have the self-esteem and guts to go ahead and do it.

For the month coming up, choose smaller, "easier" tasks to do to get you in the habit of waltzing up your limits - and going over them. They don't have to be anything special. But you need to get used to the feeling of breaking through your own self limiting beliefs - and feeling that, hooray! - you don't actually die. Those small moments of liberation will be the fuel to carry you forward and help you achieve those 12 bigger goals in time.

Finally, whittle everything down to a challenge you can do right now, today. It can be small, but do *something*. Take the risk of wearing an outfit your ex told you makes you look fat. Make a suggestion in your meeting today instead of sitting quietly and regretting it later.

The first step - a challenge for all the remaining days of this book. So - what does a challenge look like?

- Join a yoga, dance or weight lift class
- Each day make eye contact with 10 new people before they do, and don't break it first
- Talk to at least 5 strangers that day, about anything, but you initiate
- Flirt with 3 people
- Go out with less makeup or none at all if you usually do
- Do something "embarrassing"
- Visit a sauna
- Keep the lights on during sex
- Cook or eat something you have never tried before
- Call someone you've been avoiding
- Do something completely out of the ordinary, something people would never expect of you
- Give yourself a health challenge
- Go to a movie or restaurant, alone. Don't hide behind your phone, either
- Go without your TV or laptop for a day
- Try not to spend any money for the day
- Go on public transport instead of your normal way, or take a different route
- Plan a weekend day trip to somewhere you ordinarily wouldn't go
- Meditate
- Make a fool of yourself on purpose
- Ask somebody out to dinner - romantically or not

- Visit a sex shop
- Admit that you were wrong and ask someone's forgiveness
- Sleep on a different side of the bed
- Ask someone for help
- Ask someone to recommend a book or movie you would never imagine you'd seek out yourself
- Approach someone who intimidates you and compliment them
- Try a bike ride, rowboat trip or something fun and unusual
- Try a new restaurant or new cuisine
- Dance a little around your house
- Play dress up or spoil yourself to an item of clothing completely uncharacteristic of you
- Be spontaneous. Be irresponsible. Stay out all night. Why not?
- Get a spa treatment or mani/pedi
- Grow out your beard, or wear your hair differently. Maybe color it?
- Attend a new meetup group
- Buy lunch for a homeless person
- Call an old friend for an overdue catch up
- Go on a blind date, or ask a friend to plan a surprise evening where you don't know what to expect
- Eat in the dark
- Skip wearing underwear for a day. Or, wear something beautiful, sexy and luxurious
- Open up about a secret or worry that you've been holding onto. Share your fears with someone close to you
- Take a walk without knowing where you are going or for how long

For now, you can also brainstorm bigger challenges for the rest of the year...

- Travel - do it alone, outside your budget or to a place you've never considered before
- Learn a completely new skill or craft

- Hitchhike somewhere and have a spontaneous trip where you don't plan anything
- Share some of your work with the world, whatever it is. Put it out there for public scrutiny, be it a video, writing or piece of art
- Go on a hot air balloon ride
- Enroll in a martial arts class
- Join toastmasters
- Learn a musical instrument, or start singing
- Learn to paint, or dance
- Buy a motorcycle and learn to ride it
- Train hard for a marathon or similar
- Apply for a job you're not 100% qualified for
- Raise money for a charity or cause
- Crash a wedding
- ...or get married!
- Go to a nudist beach
- Write a short book or poetry collection
- Visit a swingers club or explore a long-hidden fetish
- Organize a big party or event
- Give a public talk
- Sing karaoke
- Go on silent retreat
- Ask for a raise
- Perform at an open mic night
- Learn a new language
- Start a new business
- Try therapy
- Go back to school
- Enter your work in an art show
- Confront a phobia
- Bungee jump, hang glide or skydive
- Get a piercing or tattoo
- Do a house swap

Day 5: Tackling your beliefs

At the heart of every one of our emotions is a belief. Think about that for a second. We're only ever upset when something bad happens because we have the *belief* that things *should* have turned out differently. I won't tell you that all your beliefs are wrong and that you're a crazy person. In fact, if you've been managing to feed yourself and tie your shoelaces alright thus far, you probably are doing OK in the beliefs department.

But nevertheless, it's a good idea to take some beliefs with a pinch of salt. You don't have to take anyone's word for gospel - not even your own! As you did your first challenge yesterday (and hopefully are gearing up to do another one today) your brain might have helpfully decided to jump in with a bunch of reasons why you should rather just stay in your comfort zone. It has cats! And Netflix! It's so cozy, why would you ever want to leave?

But you won't listen, because you're going to get into the habit of looking closely at the underlying beliefs behind those emotions. Usually? It's fear. Quivering, bashful, timid, over-cautious and easily frightened fear. The thing is, what's making this pansy part of you so scared is not the world out there, but the beliefs you have about the world out there, *in here*.

Lets take an example. Didi has been invited to go to a big party and wants to wear a beautiful, figure hugging yellow dress to it. The problem is she doesn't feel that she's thin or pretty or gregarious enough to pull it off, and is struggling to decide whether she should just wear something a little safer and more conservative. After all, people will stare, she'll make a fool of herself, they may judge her.

Lets look closely at all the beliefs that Didi has that she has simply assumed are true. Firstly, her belief is that only perfect, pretty and totally happy people are allowed to dress well and creatively. She also believes that when it comes to her expressing herself, the opinions of others are more valuable than her own. Lastly, if you look closely, she probably believes quite deeply that the risk of actually humiliating herself wearing something weird would be totally unbearable, and something she would rather avoid at all costs.

If she took the time to unpick these justifications to stay inside the (boring, knee-length, tasteful) comfort zone, she'd see that they weren't really all that true. She didn't need to be perfect to look good in a dress she loved, and mostly, people would respond to the fact that she was happy in it, rather than that she didn't look flawless.

While other people certainly care, in all honesty most people only give a fleeting thought to others' lives ...they just carry on stressing about their *own* as soon as possible. And as for the last belief, even if she did look ridiculous, so what? Having awful taste in clothing doesn't mean she's any less valuable as a human being, and everyone makes mistakes sometimes. Even if the "worst" thing happened - she wore the dress and regretted it - so what? Really, is it all that bad to be a human and occasionally mess up?

When Didi allows fear to guide her, she stays in her comfort zone, convinced that it's the better choice. It might feel good for a while, but she'll reach a point one day when she looks into her closet, filled with regrets. Why didn't she wear that dress more? Why did she hang back so much? Will she lie on her deathbed, wondering about all the dresses she never wore, all the fun she never had wearing whatever she damn well pleased? Maybe.

Today, as you move onto your next challenge for the week, get used to arguing with your excuses. Ask yourself what the worst case scenario is, and then say, so what? Are your assumptions really correct? Are you really being rational ...or driven by fear to stay inside your comfort zone?

Day 6: confidence is an art

As you work on your week's third challenge, whatever it is, take a moment to think of all the times in life you've felt very confident. Have a day of reminiscing and try to think back to all the times you've felt completely badass, comfortable in your skin, safe, solid and good in who you are. Do you have something in mind?

Try to think of all the things in life that have made you feel confident up to now, and how you can begin to incorporate more of those things into your everyday life. And no, you don't have to feel bad about putting "silly" things on your list like makeup or all-nighters clubbing with friends. If it made you feel confident in who you were, note it down! Maybe you put down something like...

- Going to gym and showing up the gym rats by deadlifting more than your body weight despite being 5'7

- Buying yourself a beautiful, totally unnecessary but heavenly imported body lotion that makes you smell like Aphrodite herself

- Dolling yourself up and enjoying the admiring glances of people as you waltz by them in the street, looking like you stepped out of a shampoo commercial

- Preparing a healthy and expertly made dinner for friends and family - or even yourself - and enjoying the art of the whole ceremony

- Contributing at work by beating a deadline and getting recognized for your achievements

- Hearing your partner say they love you, and appreciate everything you do for them

- Practicing a skill or talent you have and being admired for the hard work you've put into it, whether that's playing concert kazoo or stitching civil war era military costume replicas from scratch

- Speaking your mind, sharing your opinion and being creative and expressive with your own unique, possibly goofy, take on things

Since you already know that doing all these things has a positive effect on how you feel about yourself, why not go with what works and do more? Commit to going to gym more often, do more things to make your partner dote on you more, practice your hobby more, buy yourself more gadgets for your kitchen or fancy French lavender lotion. Within reason of course!

Day 7: What are you saying with your body language?

So far, we've talked about thoughts and feelings and beliefs and all the rest. But what about your body? It speaks just as clearly as the rest of you does, and it has beliefs just like the rest of you does. These *bodily beliefs* are in the form of body language.

As you move onto the rest of your week's challenges, you may already be feeling a little more pepped up, and it may be a little easier to stand taller, and hold your body differently. Luckily for us, bodies can be hacked! Yup, if you change the thoughts, the body follows, but if you change the body, the thoughts also follow. Here are some ways you can play around with fine-tuning the message your body is sending, today:

- Put your shoulders back and down. Face the world head on, not cowering. Walk into a room, literally, like you own it. Pretend you are Cleopatra or Napoleon.

- Relax your hands. People often transmit huge amounts of anxiety through fiddly, twitchy fingers. Relax your hands. Actually, relax everything.

- "Open" your face. Look people square on, with a comfortable amount of eye contact, and try not to close off your expression with tight lips, a frown or by tucking the chin under. Relax. Smile if you like.

- Use open, friendly and optimistic gestures. Keep your palms open and your torso relaxed (no twisting, folding or hunching). Use the space around you.

- Don't rush. Rushing signifies anxiety and a low-level of fear. Instead, speak slowly, clearly and with assertiveness.

- Breath. When you breath deeply and regularly, your speaking voice will be smoother and more confident. Get rid of "um" while you think, just pause instead.

- Kill all phrases like "I think" or "please" or "I'm sorry" or "Could you please maybe possibly have a look at this um yeah I'm not sure I was thinking that you could please do this thing for me if you don't mind so sorry…?" Instead, doesn't it sound more confident and assertive to simply say, "Will you do this for me? Thank you"

- When someone compliments you, smile and thank them, genuinely. No need to rush in with a "oh yes! I also like your …uh, socks" unless you actually do like them. Be graceful and move on.

Day 8: finding external motivation

Now, I know I've said that part of having solid self-confidence is not relying too seriously on other people's opinions of you, but today's exercise is about looking to others. Not for validation or permission, but for *inspiration*.

Self-improvement, confronting your demons, working on kicking your butt out of your comfort zone ...all of this can be very lonely work! It's easy to forget that other people out there are also struggling, also dealing with the same questions of their self worth, also wondering if they look like an idiot when they step out of the door every morning.

There are also amazing people out there who feel those things and get on with it anyway. Stop for a moment and see if you can think of any of them now. Who brims with calm self-confidence, assertiveness and the deep knowledge that they are a valuable, mostly awesome human being? If you can't think of anyone, try cast your mind back to a younger and pluckier you, or a time when you felt strong and free and totally accepting of all the funny little things that make you the human being you are.

Take today to reflect on these people. What do they do? How can you do the same? What's so different about them, really? Remember to keep doing your comfort zone-busting challenges!

Day 9: The fear of rejection

Lets take today to look more closely at one particular cause of low confidence and one of the most common reasons people choose to hang back, hiding their brilliant selves away from the rest of the world: rejection. Rejection can feel like death, and in a way, it kind of is. As social creatures, human beings depend on the love and acceptance of other human beings for our mental health, our sense of belonging, our identities. While this is nothing to be ashamed of, it does also mean that occasionally, we can open ourselves up to being hurt by others when they reject this need.

Most people's solution to the rejection problem is pretty simple: don't depend on other people anymore. Have you experienced this? After a bad break up, your friend might swear off the opposite sex, decide they never needed anyone anyway and to hell with it all, they can manage on their own. Fine and good, except nobody can really manage on their own forever, and eventually everyone needs to reach out, whether that's because they've locked themselves out of their apartment or because they just need a hug.

There's a better solution. Shutting down and being fiercely independent may look like confidence, but look closely. Behind all the bravado is someone who's afraid. Instead of dealing with the fact that people can hurt and reject them, they choose just to never be in the position where they can be rejected in the first place. The problem is, it's those vulnerable positions that also lead to all the good stuff - love, acceptance and compassion - and they miss out on those too.

A lot of sassy tell-it-like-it-is confident guides out there will tell you that people who reject you are *wrong*. Plain and simple. Someone rejects you? Their mistake! Their loss. Girl, he was *mad* to break up with you. Your boss just doesn't appreciate your genius, it's obvious. Your parents are morons for not supporting you in your plans.

But ...are they?

I'd like to propose a way of dealing with rejection that doesn't assume you're a completely infallible demi-god who can do no wrong and that other people are not insane. Here it is:

- Ah, so you've been rejected. Hurts like hell, doesn't it? The first step: you don't have to resist feeling crap about it. Don't be upset that you feel upset. Go with it. Rejection feels awful, just take a moment to feel awful. It's OK. Enjoy it, because...

- The next step is to take a clear look at the situation without your emotions clouding your judgment too much. Ask yourself if *you* are really being rejected at all. If a person turns you down romantically because someone better came along or because they just weren't feeling it, that's not really a rejection of who you are. To prove this to yourself, think of a person you weren't keen to date or get to know but who you felt sure was a fabulous and worthwhile person nonetheless. See? Likewise, if someone appears to lash out at you or turn you down for reasons that have nothing to do with you, take a moment to notice that. Don't take it personally, even though it may be difficult. If your boss doesn't like your proposal, well, he rejected your proposal, not you. Relax. You can make another proposal.

- Of course, I'm not going to sugar coat things for you: sometimes, you really will be rejected. You can be all the glorious fabulous loveliness that you are right now and somebody could look at you and think, "nah." If this is the case for you, wonderful, this is one of the best exercises to whip out a rock-solid sense of self. Let's say a new partner breaks up with you and explicitly does so because they find your habits and lifestyle a constant irritation and your personality on par with a brain-damaged duck. They reject *you*. Damn. Well, ask yourself two questions: Is it true? What can you do about it?

- If the person happens to be completely wrong about you, then, so what? Move on with your life.

- If the person happens to be a little tiny bit possibly maybe right, then your challenge is to see what you can do about it. Some people make the best changes to their lives after someone has the courage to tell them the hard truth. Do you care about making improvements? What can you do?

- This last bit is the most important - what if you *can't* change the thing you were rejected over? If somebody rejects you because of where you were born or how tall you are or some other thing that's beyond your control, then you only waste time worrying further about it. You are who you are. Even the bad things. Self-love is easy when other people can love you for the same things - but most powerful when you have the courage to love those things that even others can't.

Day 10: Taking stock

Well! By now you would have completed 5 different exercises to gently push you out of your comfort zone and into an exciting new zone where you can start growing more and more confident. Now, don't worry if you don't feel like this is such an achievement, especially if you erred on the side of small and doable rather than anything that would make you die from cringing too hard.

But these small tasks are important. Why? Because they give you a constant chance to prove to yourself that you can push yourself, that you can do new things and that you can be someone different. In fact, many smaller activities only means more opportunities for you to press against your limits a little and see that for the most part, everything is fine! You are still alive!

But, don't stop there. Now that you're getting the hang of pushing yourself, go a little further. Why not? Keep coming back to your list of challenges, and keep picking new ways to gently push yourself.

Day 11: Getting over embarrassment

Do you cover your mouth when you laugh in public? Do you say "sorry" when someone steps on your toe in the bus station? Do you blush if you trip while walking in the streets and immediately worry about who saw you and what they'll think?

Embarrassment is the younger, more annoying cousin of plain old shame. Embarrassment is like a tiny policeman we carry in our minds that keeps reminding us to watch out just in case our real selves break free and everyone sees us for *who we really are*, cue horror music. Think about this for a second - what's so terrible about our real, uncensored selves anyway?

So we live in fear of saying something wrong, or making a fool of ourselves, of everyone turning to look and see, maybe even laugh at us. But again, what's so bad about occasionally making a fool of yourself, or of being perceived as less than perfect?

The next time you goof up in a big way, don't turn a deep shade of crimson and start looking for a hole to crawl into. Have a laugh at yourself, shrug your shoulders, say "we all make mistakes" and get on with it. Guaranteed is that most people won't remember your faux pas, or even notice it in the first place.

Day 12: Forget about yourself

Let's stay on the topic of other people for a moment. Often, when we're eaten up by guilt and shame and self-doubt and all those other uncomfortable things, there's one thing we forget about: everyone else. It's weird, actually. We all worry ourselves to death about other people's opinions of us, but if you can't spare a thought for what other people are doing because you're too busy stressing about yourself, what makes you think they aren't doing the same?

Ah, you say, but *what if I am totally judging other people?*

Well, thank you for being honest. The truth is that our judgments of others often reflect the way we feel about ourselves. You can be sure that the person who is super-harsh about someone else uses similar standards for themselves. Those who judge often fear the same judgment being turned on them, and those who have the courage to accept others often do so because they learnt how to accept themselves first.

What I'm saying is that these things are connected, and that you can't become more accepting and compassionate with yourself without also getting a little of that love on others ...and vice versa.

If you find yourself saying bitchy things like, "I can't believe he's humiliating himself like that" or "that's a stupid idea, I don't know why she brought it up", try turning the same judgment on yourself. Is it really yourself that you feel ashamed and unaccepting of? In fact, is the person you're judging doing something you wish you could do if you weren't so unconfident?

The next time you feel jealous or envious of someone, practice praising that person instead. Be confident enough in yourself to recognize the good in others when you see it, even if it's about something that you yourself are still working on. So, if you think a woman who passes you in the street looks ridiculous with her haircut, turn it around. Tell yourself that *you* look good today, and have nice hair. Tell yourself that it's OK to do whatever the hell you want with your hair, and that means *you* too.

This may seem silly at first, but just try it. It often doesn't take much digging to uncover the real reason we are judgmental and critical of others, and it usually has nothing to do with them! Bear this in mind the next time someone is disapproving of you for what seems like no reason.

Day 13: Shame

We've dealt a little with worry and embarrassment, but what about shame? What about that deep, ugly, painful feeling inside that you are, in reality, a *bad person*. Shame is one of the worst things we can feel on this earth, because it undermines everything that we are and do. Shame means believing not only that we have done wrong, but that we *are* wrong, and many people walk around with shame so deep it would take your breath away to witness it.

Shame can come about from years of conditioning from those we love, or from our parents and teachers. It can come from making mistakes and never finding the courage to forgive ourselves. Sometimes, the shame we feel is not even ours, and is instead handed onto us from someone else. Shame hurts. Shame is pretty serious.

So - lets not dwell on it! Other books can help you get to the root of shame if you feel this is something that is massively holding you back, but to be honest, there is only way to let go of shame: just let it go. Really. Maybe it sounds glib, but let it go. Look at those dark, scary, unhappy thoughts and simply say, "I'm letting you go now." That's all. Repeat this every time you feel shame bubbling up.

Day 14: Making mistakes like a pro

It's a myth that confident people don't make mistakes. In fact, they probably make a lot *more* mistakes than anyone else, because they're not holding back. Here's something scary: when you actively try to push outside of your comfort zone, you up the risk that you make a mistake. Maybe you bite off more than you can chew, maybe you try something truly moronic, or figure out you can't be trusted to walk a 80 lb Labrador after all. Maybe you take the risk and make an ass of yourself. Ouch, Now what?

Well, when it happens (notice I say *when* and not *if*) you're going to do a few of the following things:

- You're going to say, "people make mistakes. I'm a people. I make mistakes. It's all OK"

- You're going to try and laugh at yourself. One of the best ways to put little glitches into perspective is to see them for what they are: kind of funny

- You're going to refrain from using this as evidence that you should stop trying anything new. In fact, you're going to use it as proof that you're on the right track. After all, making mistakes means you're really in new territory, which is exactly what you want

- Once you've gotten over your bruised ego and your cheeks are not so red anymore, take a deep breath and see what you've learnt. How can you be better? Is this the right direction to pursue?

- Don't let a failure be the *last* thing you do. Get back into things, and try again. Don't think of yourself as a performer or someone in a competition, think of yourself as a scientist who's gathering data about *what works*

- Find a mentor or inspirational figure that also failed a whole bunch but managed to be successful anyway. Ask yourself what they would do in your situation

- A good technique: ask yourself, "will any of this matter in a year?" and if not, then scale back your stress and worry about it. Focus on the important things

- Lastly, if you've messed up and hurt others, well, your challenge is to say sorry - properly. Apologize, don't dwell on how bad *you* feel, then explain exactly what you're going to do to make sure it doesn't happen again

Today's exercise: be free and easy in admitting you are wrong (a challenge in itself!) and then - the fun part - forgive yourself for messing up. Failure is a gift. It's a clue to how you can be better. Be glad to fail.

Day 15: Fear of the unknown

What exactly *is* the unknown? Well, uh ...nobody knows. That's kinda the point. But into that big empty space, we often end up projecting our biggest, darkest, nastiest fears. There is a saying that goes, "the thing you are most afraid of has actually already happened to you" and what it points to is the fact that most of the time, our stress and worry about the unknown is overblown.

Outside of your comfort zone = the unknown. Could be amazing, could be a kick in the head, who knows? Are you willing to take the risk? With confidence, comes the strength of character to know that you can and will take on that risk - and *you'll be OK, whatever happens*. Confidence in yourself is not the knowledge that you can never fail, or never be hurt. It's the knowledge that you have the strength of will and character to shrug it off and say, "yeah so what - bring it on."

Yesterday, I asked you to get comfortable with saying "I messed up" and today, I'm going to ask you to try and get comfortable with another three tricky words: "I don't know". It's tempting to want to understand everything, because knowledge of a thing gives us *control*. Today, let go of that control and be happy with a bit of mystery.

A funny thing happens though, when you stop trying to grasp at explaining things: they become less scary. The next time someone asks you something like, "what are you doing with your life?" instead of launching into an explanation that makes you seem like you're perfectly in control, have the guts to say, "Well, I actually don't know."

What's so bad about that? The great thing about admitting that things are unknown means you are still open to explore, still receptive to new information. You're outside of your comfort zone, where all the magic happens.

If you're stressing about the future or some unknown variables, ask yourself a few questions.

- Is everything OK, *right now*?

- What's the worst that could happen? Is that really so bad?

- Is it the end of the world if I don't understand 100% what is happening here?

You could meditate or stress or try to pin down complicated situations. Or you could let them be as complicated as you wanted, without feeling threatened or afraid. Today, try to let nagging questions go unanswered. It's not so scary, is it?

Day 16: trying on different frames

Today, a simple, but profound exercise. The imagery of moving outside of or away from your comfort zone makes you think of growth as something *more*. But sometimes growth is just *different*. Sometimes, nothing needs to change in a situation other than your thoughts about it. Today, play with language a bit and reframe what you say. Challenge yourself to see things in a different light. Try on different perspectives like you might try on different jackets.

You could say, "I'm failing hard and people can tell" or you could say, "I can encourage others by showing that I'm not afraid to be vulnerable."

You could say, "People are all judgmental and harsh" or you could say, "We're all struggling to accept ourselves. I'm going to be brave and accept myself anyway."

You could say, "I don't deserve to feel good about myself because I suck so bad" or you could say, "I'm still working on it, and I'll get there."

Day 17: Reflect

From one perspective, trying to improve your level of self-confidence is a pretty simple, almost boring concept. From another perspective, you're doing something bold, courageous and a little scary, something that could change you completely. Take today to reflect on yourself and how you've grown and changed over the last few days. Go back to your original confidence 'rating". Has anything changed...?

Day 18: The importance of self care

We've seen that at its root, low self-confidence is a nasty cocktail of shame, embarrassment and the deep-down feeling that when it comes down to it, you aren't worth very much. If something isn't worth much, then you don't take care of it, right?

Today, practice treating yourself like you *are already valuable*. Don't try to justify to yourself why you deserve a bit of pampering, you don't have to "earn" it or feel guilty, do it just because you are a valuable thing, and valuable things need to be cared for. That's it.

Take a step back and look at yourself as a thing that ought to be cared for.

- Are you eating well?

- Do you sleep enough?

- Do you have people around you who are supportive and loving?

- Do you have work and hobbies that fulfill you intellectually?

- Do you feel spiritually safe and secure?

- Do you take care of yourself when you're ill?

- Are you staying away from addictive and harmful substances?

- Are you staying away from harmful people?

- Do you have joy and humor and happiness in your life?

- Are you safe and do you have adequate stress relief techniques?

Choose one thing today to do to take care of yourself. Don't think of it as "spoiling" or a "treat". Think of it as completely normal and expected. When you are confident, it's natural for you to want to take care of yourself!

Day 19: Confident expression

For many people, their lack of confidence shows itself in limited, doubtful expression. These are the secret artists among us, the quiet ones hiding all their brilliant skill and fascinating ideas and perspectives behind a veil of ordinariness. Why? Fear of rejection. Fear of the unknown.

Are you one of these people who constantly thinks, "I should have said something. I didn't express myself clearly." Being confident means not allowing your true self to go unspoken and unshown to the world. Yeah, it's possible nobody likes what you're offering, but the value is in speaking your truth, whatever it happens to be.

Don't be a secret artist. Express yourself - and take a risk by making it mean something. Join a writing group, show your artwork to somebody, or speak your mind when you have a novel thought. Don't do it with the hope that you will be praised. Let go of others' opinions and speak up just because it feels good to let others know who you are.

Day 20: The gift of vulnerability

"Brittle things break before they bend"

A "brittle thing" is an ego propped up with the validation of others, with achievements and external recognition. It looks alright until that recognition isn't there anymore, and then it crumbles. One small attack and it breaks to pieces. Instead of being super strong, unyielding and stiff, try to be flexible instead. Be OK with making mistakes, with being unsure and being a little vulnerable.

Can you get hurt? Sure. But that makes the rewards of the risk so much sweeter. If you have the courage to be vulnerable, you may find that you inspire others to let down their guard, to be human and fallible, too. When you have the guts to be vulnerable, you realize that your fears were never really that scary in the first place, and that even if the worst thing happens, you can survive and grow from it.

Ways you can be stronger by being more vulnerable

- Ask for help

- Admit when you're wrong

- Don't be afraid to express negative emotions

- Lean on someone for a while

- Be grateful for everything that you have

- Be authentically what you are

- Try to accept your flaws instead of railing against them

- Ask for forgiveness

- … and forgive those who have hurt you

Day 21: Cultivating self-awareness

Negative self-talk is only dangerous when you mistake it for cold hard truth. Look at the fluttering in your head for what it really is: noise. Irrelevant. Not any more significant or trustworthy than a gargle in your stomach or a twitch in your eye. Most people are surprisingly nice to each other, when you compare it to *how we talk to ourselves* every day, in our minds. That constant stream of negative self-talk is useless, and the sooner you can learn to notice it when it happens, the easier it will be to say, "yes, well frankly that's a load of crap" and move on.

Today, watch yourself closely for every time you put yourself down, or tell yourself why you can't or shouldn't do something, or that you are not good enough to get the things you want. Just noticing these thoughts at all can be a mission, but once you notice them, challenge yourself. Is it really true? What other perspectives are you not thinking of?

If you feel like you never have any self-talk, well, I hate to tell you this, but this probably means you've just accepted your negative self talk as truth. Questions those assumptions. Are they true? Really?

On the other hand, if you feel like your mind is constantly swirling with negativity and that you can't believe how dark it is in there - fantastic! Fear means you are doing the work, going outside your comfort zone and adapting ...even if it doesn't feel like progress.

Awareness is merely shining a light on yourself, and having a look. Try not to judge what you see there, or wonder what it "should" be. Be curious, and gentle, and compassionate with yourself. Take a step back and ask if you ever really deserve to be treated like a thing that is worthless or undeserving. Where did you learn this attitude? Has it helped you at all? What would your life look like if you dropped it...?

From here on: the 1-year comfort zone challenge!

We have been on this self-confidence challenge for 3 weeks now, which is not a lot of time in some ways, and an eternity in others. What happens after day 21, you ask? Well, a lot. That's because self-confidence and the development of deep self-love and acceptance is an ongoing, never-ending *becoming*, a thing that never stops growing and changing and developing.

Haul out your list of one-year challenges that you drew up in the earlier part of this book. It's OK if you look at some of those things and think, "oh God, what was I thinking!" Very often, you'll find something on the list that was only ever put there because it seemed like it "should" be there. It's OK - just take it off. Adjust any that seemed overly ambitious - or even too easy now!

As you take stock, try not to judge, or give yourself a score - as long as you've made some sort of progress and movement, congratulations, your time spent on this challenge has been worth it! When you get stuck on goal-oriented thinking, you can lose track of the magic of the process. If you've achieved something you never imagined you could, take a moment to feel proud - but don't stop there! Remember that feeling the next time you tell yourself, "I can't do this." Because you can!

55610803R00029

Made in the USA
Lexington, KY
28 September 2016